IT'S TIME TO EAT
CANNED TUNA

It's Time to Eat CANNED TUNA

Walter the Educator

Silent King Books
A WhichHead Entertainment Imprint

It's Time to Eat CANNED TUNA is a collectible early learning book by Walter the Educator suitable for all ages belonging to Walter the Educator's Time to Eat Book Series. Collect more books at WaltertheEducator.com

USE THE EXTRA SPACE TO TAKE NOTES AND DOCUMENT YOUR MEMORIES

CANNED TUNA

It's time to eat, it's time to share,

It's Time to Eat

Canned

Tuna

Canned tuna's ready, we'll prepare!

Open the can with a twist or a snap,

What's inside is a tasty trap!

Soft and flaky, it smells like the sea,

A treat for you, a treat for me.

Mix it up, or eat it plain,

Canned tuna fun is here again!

On a sandwich or in a wrap,

Tuna's tasty, it's no mishap.

Add some veggies, crunchy and sweet,

Canned tuna makes a meal complete.

Stir it in pasta, make it shine,

Or with some crackers, it's just fine.

A squirt of lemon, a sprinkle of spice,

Every bite is oh so nice!

It's Time to Eat

Canned

Tuna

For lunch or dinner, or even a snack,

Canned tuna gives you what you lack.

Packed with protein, healthy and good,

A little fish power for your mood!

Mix it with mayo, or keep it dry,

Add it to salads, it's worth a try.

Canned tuna's handy, it's quick to make,

A meal in minutes, for goodness' sake!

Pretend you're fishing, cast your line,

Catch some tuna, it's snack time!

Reel it in and give it a bite,

Canned tuna's flavor is just right.

From ocean waves to your kitchen dish,

Canned tuna's here, your wishful fish.

It's simple, yummy, and oh so neat,

The perfect treat for us to eat.

It's time to eat, it's time to share,

Canned tuna's ready, we'll prepare!

Open the can with a twist or a snap,

It's Time to Eat

Canned

Tuna

What's inside is a tasty trap!

So grab a fork and dig right in,

Canned tuna time will make you grin.

It's tasty, fun, and easy to share,

A little can with flavors rare!

ABOUT THE CREATOR

Walter the Educator is one of the
pseudonyms for Walter Anderson.
Formally educated in Chemistry,
Business, and Education, he is an
educator, an author, a diverse
entrepreneur, and he is the son
of a disabled war veteran.
"Walter the Educator" shares his
time between educating and creating.
He holds interests and owns several
creative projects that entertain,
enlighten, enhance, and educate,
hoping to inspire and motivate you.
Follow, find new works, and stay
up to date with Walter the Educator™

at WaltertheEducator.com

Milton Keynes UK
Ingram Content Group UK Ltd.
UKHW010227111224
452348UK00011B/550